There Still Is HOPE

SIX PRACTICAL KEYS FOR GETTING OVER LIFE'S DISTRACTIONS AND OBSTACLES

Montreal D. Martin

There Still Is
HOPE

Montreal D. Martin

LOWBAR
PUBLISHING COMPANY

Montreal D. Martin, Author

Printed in the United States of America in 2012
© 2012 by Lowbar Publishing Company

ISBN: 978-0-9827151-6-1
    Lowbar Publishing Company Nashville,
    Tennessee 37204
    615-972-2842
    E-mail: Lowbarpublishingcompany@gmail.com
    Web site: www.Lowbarbookstore.com

Editor/Copy Editor: Honey B. Higgins
Layout Designer: Norah S. Branch
Graphic Art and Book Cover Designer: Norah S. Branch

For speaking engagements, workshops, and seminars, here is how you may contact the author:

    Lowbar Publishing Company 905 South
    Douglas Avenue Nashville, TN 37204
    Phone: (615) 972-2842
    Lowbarpublishingcompany@gmail.com

All rights reserved under the International Copyright Law. Contents and book cover cannot be reproduced in whole or in part in any form without the expressed written consent of the author and/or publisher.

"Montreal encourages his readers to respond in the same way that Paul spoke to Timothy: 'Pursue righteousness, godliness, faith, love, endurance and gentleness. Fight the good fight of faith. Take hold of the eternal life' (1 Timothy 6:11-12a, NIV). In his day-to-day actions, he inspires those around him by humbly pointing to God as the answer to life."
—C. J. Behnke, MSE

"[In] *There Still Is Hope*, Martin writes for all those who suffer with the issues of this thing called LIFE—taking the obstacles of daily living (the feelings of failure, defeat, anger) and transferring that energy into a way of restoration, success, [and] accomplishments. Whether you are beginning your walk of faith or have journeyed with the Lord for many years, these clear inspirations will show you how to transform your life and your feelings toward life's events. Through this book, Martin will grab your attention and remind you of the fullness of divine power and the joy of the Lord!"
—Andre` R. Trice
Minister of Music, Mt. Hopewell Baptist Church

CONTENTS

Foreword viii

Acknowledgments.. ix

Chapter 1
    Introduction..1

Chapter 2
    Key #1—He Wants It All: Relinquish Yourself to God 6

Chapter 3
    Key #2—We Fall Down:
        Reaching to God for Forgiveness......................16

Chapter 4
    Key #3—He Saw the Best in Me:
        Realizing God's Favor upon Your Life 26

Chapter 5
    Key #4—Never Would Have Made It:
        Recognize the Source of Your Strength 36

Chapter 6
    Key #5—Prayed Up: Regular Rapport with God 44

Chapter 7
    Key #6—Smile: Retain Your Faith 53

Conclusion 62

About the Author..64

FOREWORD

I met Montreal Martin in 2010. Montreal was one of the young preachers that attended our "Saturday Night Youth Services." He was and still is a very soft-spoken and well-mannered young man. After reading his manuscript, I can personally testify that he is the personification of his book.

The book chronicles a life of hopelessness that leads to incarceration. Yet, while facing the possibility of years of incarceration, he rediscovers the Christ that he met at the age of nine. As I read the manuscript and reflected upon the young man that I have come to know, I am filled with a hope that many more young boys and girls can experience the same transformation in Christ.

This book is a parent's dream, inasmuch as it speaks to the challenges that many teens and parents face daily. I strongly recommend this book as a resource of inspiration and transformation for every person who works with youth and young adults—who asks the question, Where is hope? *There Still Is Hope* is a book that desires a place in your library.

Bishop Calvin C. Barlow Jr., Pastor
Second Missionary Baptist Church
1000 Halcyon Avenue
Nashville, TN 37204

ACKNOWLEDGMENTS

I give honor and praise to the Most High God, who is the Head of my life; I know that without Him, I would not be who and where I am today. I thank the Lord for blessing me beyond measure, and for protecting me.

To Toni L. Martin, whom I have grown to call "mother"... because that is what you have been to me ever since you took me into your home: *I want to thank you for your unconditional love, support, and patience during the most challenging years of my life; thank you for being the Woman of God that you are—I love you.* In addition, I want to thank my biological mother, Sheila M. Martin, and father, Vanshae Thompson; thank you both for everything: the good times we have shared, and the ones still to come. I love you dearly.

To my great host of brothers, sisters, aunts, uncles, cousins, nieces, nephews, friends, and friends of the family: I really would like to express my sincere appreciation for everything each of you has done in my life—I love you all.

Next, I would like to thank all the faculty and staff at Rawhide Boys Ranch; and although I am not a resident anymore, as the Alumnus Motto goes, "Once a Rawhide guy...always a Rawhide guy!" To John and Jan Gillespie (Founders), Bart and Cherri Starr (Co-founders), John Solberg (Executive Director), Jeff and Brenda Stumpf (my house parents), C. J. and Lisa Behnke, Roy Cobbs, Jim Waters, and all the former and current Rawhide faculty and staff who were all valuable presences in my life: You all enriched my life in many different ways—not because it was your job, but because you all actually care for every young man who comes to Rawhide, regardless of his past. You recognize what God is currently doing in the now, which gives hope. Keep your fire burning for the Lord and know that He will give you all the strength that is needed; He will keep pouring out His blessings upon you. I also extend thanks to every donor who has supported Rawhide; your donations really help change lives. God bless you all.

To all the men and women of God who have taken me under their wings in order to mentor me and pour into my ministry: May God continue to shine on and anoint each of you.

Special thanks are extended to the following people:

Bishop Lawrence L. Kirby and the St. Paul M.B. Church family (Racine, Wisconsin), for everything you all have done for me, thus helping me to grow into the person I am today. Bishop Kirby, thank you for your leadership, guidance, and mentorship, and for being a surrogate father figure to me. Your ambition, intellect, and nobility exemplify your character and the man of God you are; you display the favor of God that is upon you, through your obedience and humility. May God continue to bless you and your family—I love you.

Pastor Duane M. Sleet and First Baptist Church (of Far Rockaway, New York), thank you all for the love and support that you have shown me during my internship with you as Youth Pastor; you all have become my extended family. Pastor Sleet, thank you again for providing me with the opportunity to grow as a young minister and man. Thank you for sharing your life experiences with me, helping me to learn how to advance myself in ministry and life.

Pastor Joe Games and Providence M.B. Church of Milwaukee, Wisconsin, thank you for everything you have done over the years—but most of all, thank you for believing in me and supporting my education. Pastor Games, thank you for being a pioneer in believing in the "young preacher" through your prayers and support. God bless.

Pastor Darrell Drumwright and Temple Church of Nashville, Tennessee, thanks for having open arms and taking me in as your own when I arrived in Nashville to attend school. Bless you all.

Pastor T. A. Knapp (Mrs. Knapp and girls) and Mount Calm M.B. Church of Minden, Louisiana, thank you for welcoming me into your homes and for all your support over the years; it was your prayers and donations that got me through school, when I had just enough to get by. Thanks.

Rev. Dr. Forrest E. Harris, president of American Baptist College, and its faculty, staff, and past and present students—thank you all for your leadership and dedication to the students, and for teaching me to light a flame that will last forever. I will always love thee, Alma Mater, the school I cherish so…

Kurt Wahlen, former chief of the Racine PoliceDepartment—thank you for your prayers and support over the years; may God continue to bless you and your family.

To the brethren of the Alpha Iota Nu Fraternity Inc. of Hoi Adelphoi, thank you all for uplifting me as you climbed, and assisting me in order to ensure that I kept my "DOT"; bless each and every one of you. Keep lifting!

For those whose names may not have been mentioned, just know that I really appreciate everything that you have done for me which allowed me to grow; thanks for the contributions that you have made to my life—I love you all.

Shalom

Because of Him

Chapter 1

Introduction

Can you imagine a time in your life when you were on the road of HOPELESSNESS? Perhaps you cannot do so at this very moment, but I know I can—as a matter of fact, it seemed as though I called that road "home" many a time. I can recall a time when I was at the Racine Juvenile Detention Center, awaiting trial for the charges brought against me. I remember lying in my bunk one day after coming back from meeting with my attorney; there I lay, riddled with all types of built-up emotions—one of which was the hopelessness that seemed to overshadow the other emotions I was feeling.

It was after lunch when my attorney came to visit me; we greeted each other and got down to business. The first words out of her mouth were, "I have some good news and I have some bad news; which would you like first, Mr. Martin?" Of course, I opted to hear the bad news first, thinking that it could not possibly be that bad—but that thought quickly changed when she told me that I was being waived into the adult court, which meant that I was going to be charged as an adult at the age of fourteen (going on fifteen): for carjacking while carrying a concealed weapon; for OVWOC (operating vehicle without owner's consent); for fleeing and eluding an officer; and for obstruction—all of which were felonies.

When she told me those things, I remember my heart feeling as though it had dropped to the pit of my stomach. I began to panic, asking her why this was happening, what they were going to do to me, and what this meant for my life. All I could remember were the words of the judge from my prior appearances in court, warning me that if he was to see me back in his courtroom, he was going to see to it that I would not be seeing it (or anything else) for a long time. My attorney attempted to calm me down and tried to assure me that everything was going to be all right. At that time, I was not even trying to hear it; all I was trying to hear was someone yelling my name, telling me to wake up—indicating that I was just having a bad dream. After I realized that I was indeed in the real world, I calmed down a bit. She then began to present me with the good news, which at that point I did not care to hear; but I allowed her to speak her peace anyway. She proceeded to tell me that I could plead insanity and possibly get the charges reduced and/or dismissed.

To this day, I remember looking that attorney in her face and saying, "That's it? You call that good news? That isn't good news." She told me to think about it and that she was going to check back with me later on in the week. As I was being escorted back to my dayroom, I remember walking down those dimly lit halls in total silence; other inmates and staff who passed by were trying to speak to me—saying hello—but I just kept walking, drowning out the noise. At that time, I was in no mood to be spoken to nor did I want to talk to anybody, not even to myself. After being led to the dayroom, I immediately entered my cell and lay on my bunk with the unnumbered thoughts running through my head in every direction—one being, "What now?" There I was left with myself, feeling abandoned and as though I had nothing to live for.

I could not picture myself inside of a prison. From the many stories I had heard and from what I had witnessed myself while visiting incarcerated family members, it was a place where I did not want to go. While wrapped up in my emotions, I remembered the words of all the preachers, Sunday school teachers, VBS leaders, and, of course, Grandma (R.I.P. Grandma "Dot"), reminding me that I could go to Jesus at anytime and for anything, because I was a child of God. Those words replayed repeatedly in my head until finally, I dropped to my knees and began to pray to God, asking Him to come into my situation and save me. After I picked myself up off the floor—feeling somewhat relieved—I then looked over at my desk and noticed a *Daily Bread* devotional lying there. So I picked it up, flipped through the pages until I reached the date of that particular day, and read the story and Scripture (which was Romans 10:9): "If you confess with your mouth,'Jesus [Christ] is Lord,' and believe in your heart that God raised him from the dead, you will be saved" (NIV).

I could recall committing my life to Jesus at the age of eleven—but were my motives really genuine back then? Or, was I just going with the flow and treating Jesus as though He were a fresh pair of new kicks that had just come out: all right at the moment, until a new pair would hit the market and then in the closet He went to collect dust? So, there I was again—confessing and recommitting myself to Him, this time wholeheartedly and genuinely.

I really could care less about what others would say about my recommitting my life to Jesus while incarcerated. You can call it "jailhouse Christianity" all you want, but what you do not realize is that God may put us in situations and places where we do not want to be, just to get our attention—trust me, I am a living witness. Though I had been raised in the church (I attended with my grandmother), it was not necessarily where I wanted to spend my time. But when she began to have health issues, I started to attend a neighborhood church: St. Paul Missionary Baptist Church.

As I "graced" the neighborhood functions with my presence (such as the Vacation Bible School functions, The Awana Club, and The Godfathers Program [Mentoring Program]), I thought I was doing God a favor by being the light in my community and family—but really, I was just giving the church a bad name, particularly the black church. I was just going through the motions and rituals of what I thought a Christian must do to be considered a "Christian." Though it had probably been explained to me before, I had not taken it seriously—that I had been saved through faith, and not because of anything that I had done or could do. So there I was in my cell—a born-again believer. I could tell that something was going on inside of me, because I just felt so different; and then it seemed as though my worries were gone.

Well, I was making my bunk two days later when my name was called over the intercom in the dayroom, which told me to be ready in five minutes because I had a visitor. I thought to myself, *It is not after dinner or the weekend, so who could possibly be coming to see me?* After looking at the clock, I deduced that the only possible two individuals who could be paying me a visit were my agent or my attorney—and as I had figured, it was my attorney. We greeted each other in the usual fashion and then got down to business. As with our previous meeting, she promptly initiated the conversation with, "I have some good news and I have some bad news; which would you like first?" I do not know if she thought that my being detained was a game or something, but I sure was not about to play; so I told her that it did not matter which came first.

My attorney opted to tell me the "good news" first. She said that the District Attorney's office had devised a deal for me in the form of a plea bargain—that I be waived back into the juvenile court system by pleading guilty to the charges, and that I complete this program (serious juvenile offender program). This would mean that I would spend five years in the custody of the State of Wisconsin. My attorney further advised me that the deal was a good deal, considering the fact that I had prior convictions under my belt, dating back to my being eleven years of age. Plus, the bad news was that I had passed the psychological evaluation, meaning that I could either take the plea or get charged as an adult. Needless to say, I agreed to the SJO Program.

As I reflect on the emotions I was feeling back then, I am reminded of when President Barack Obama got elected as the United States' first African-American president. The nation had let out a huge sigh of relief, because of the hope that President Obama had given to the American people. President Obama related to the people, simply because of who he was and where he had come from. As I read his biography and book, I realized that his story is our story: with a mama from Kansas and a daddy from Kenya, who had gotten a divorce while he was a baby—and as a result, he was left estranged from his dad. Sound familiar? Yes, the details of the story may differentiate, but the struggle is the same. And it is through his having overcome this struggle that he offers hope to the American people who share a similar fate. Thank you, President Obama.

Hope. What is hope? My dear friend Webster would define *hope* as "to desire with expectation of obtainment." What did I really want out of my life that seemed to be out of reach? Did it seem as though my hope had been snatched from me? These are the questions that flooded my mind day in and day out—until I found these keys and put them to good use. If any of us ponder these questions, then this is the book to read. This book will give curious minds the keys to unlocking true destiny, and will lift the veil which is hiding the hope that awaits all of us.

I keep it real, since doing so is the only way to get through life.

Chapter 2

He Wants It All: Relinquish Yourself to God

Oftentimes in our lives, we tend to have "half-steppin'" spirits: we "commit" to something, but we do not give it our all (our best efforts). In the long run, however, we end up wishing that we had given it our all—only after all is said and done (after it seems to be too late). If we are really honest with ourselves, we can probably testify and admit that once upon a time, we have "half stepped" with God. I know that when *I* began my walk with Christ, I was "half steppin'"; I wanted to walk with Christ but, at the same time, I wanted to "do me." This meant that I would acknowledge Christ as my God and personal Savior (and all that this recognition entailed), yet I would still do what I needed and wanted to do in order to survive in life—or so I rationalized in my mind.

During this so-called walk with Christ, I was conducting myself the only way I knew how: by putting my street survival tactics and knowledge to work. I was just communicating with God whenever I needed Him for something and/or was asking Him for

His forgiveness—because I knew that I was getting ready to do wrong or had already done wrong. At that time, I did not realize that I was actually selling myself short; when it was all said and done, I was giving myself the short end of the stick.

By the grace of God, my selfish and disobedient ways landed me in a place where I did not want to be: Ethan Allen Boys School—a secured correctional facility. The judge had sentenced me to complete this five-year Serious Juvenile Offender Program (SJO); it was a program geared toward rehabilitating delinquent youth who had committed serious crimes, preparing them to reenter society by changing the way they think, thus altering the decision-making processes which lead to their actions. This program was broken down into two different classes: choices and changes. You must successfully graduate from both classes in order to be considered for release.

> At that time, I did not realize that I was actually selling myself short; when it was all said and done, I was giving myself the short end of the stick.

I was not very excited about going to a place where I was going to spend five years of my prime; I was nervous yet at the same time grateful, because I could have ended up in a far worse facility. I must admit, my first thirty days there were a living hell—being there was literally living torture. All new inmates were placed in this cottage (Marquette), which was the intake and reception cottage. All inmates were required to spend 22.25 hours of 24 hours inside of their 9'x10' living quarters (room); I was allotted one hour for recreation, and forty-five minutes for breakfast, lunch, and dinner (broken down into fifteen-minute increments, which also was the time to brush my teeth and use the bathroom). Fortunately I had a roommate, so we passed the time by playing two-handed spades and other card games; or we would reminisce about the streets where we grew up and about how if we had things to do differently, we would.

I had arrived at Ethan Allen Boys School in the summer, which was the time of the year when we were able to open our windows. The inmates would take advantage of this opportunity, "fishing" items back and forth from room to room; or an inmate would communicate with another through his window, yelling out his room number or nickname (if he was known by one). I felt sorry for the ones who did not have a "roomie"; I do not know what I would have done—had I not had one. It was during my time in this cottage that my feeling of hopelessness kicked in again. I felt all alone and abandoned yet again. I had never been so far away from the city (Racine) in which I grew up or my family for that length of time; I felt so disconnected from the things and people with whom/which I was familiar. Although I spent over six months inside of the detention center, I had been somewhat at ease—but I then started to feel anxious because I did not know what to expect, since my stint at Marquette was ending. The thirty days that I spent there had allowed me to think about a lot of things. After my thirty days in that hellhole, I finally went to the place where I was going to endure the balance of my sentence—Draper—the cottage which housed all of the SJOs (Serious Juvenile Offenders). After hearing the stories about Draper during my stay in Marquette, I could not wait to get there. Most of what I had heard was true: the older guys were housed in Draper, which offered a more relaxed and mature setting than the others.

The longest stretch of time an inmate would spend in his room was about eight to ten hours; outside the confines of his room, he was either attending school, working, at the HU (Health Unit), in his program class, or participating in some type of recreational activity in the dayroom. These were the things which characterized the typical stay in the Serious Juvenile Offender Program.

Well, the time had finally come for my second OJOR (Office of Juvenile Offender Review), which entailed meeting with my probation officer, my assigned reviewer, and my case manager from Ethan Allen. During this review, they would meet with me to discuss my stay, whether I had perpetrated any infractions or had needed any disciplinary action to be taken against me, my program and educational status, and my possible release. As with my first OJOR, I was given another 180 days until I would get my next OJOR; I really was not surprised about that ruling. My third and fourth OJORs came and went—and with each, I was told I had another 180 days until my next review.

Around the time of my fifth OJOR, I had successfully completed the SJO Program and obtained my high school diploma. As a result of my completion of the required programs and my good behavior, I was introduced to another program: the About Face Boot Camp of Rawhide Boys Ranch—a Christian-based program. I will never forget the day when Lisa Behnke, who was the About Face's Social Worker, interviewed prospective cadets to enter into the program. I was nervous during the interview but, at the same time, excited, because there we were, discussing a possible release. Lisa's awesome smile and excitement/energy for the Lord as well as the program got me pumped about a program I knew nothing about. But if the experience was anything like she had described it, then I definitely did not mind being a part of it.

After spending almost three years in Ethan Allen, I was super excited about going to Rawhide. This program was to last for 120 days (four calendar months)—if successfully completed. I was housed in the Carriage House, which accommodated the About Face Program; there were approximately twenty guys living in the house when I arrived.

I tell the following story every time I give my testimony: I remember when I first arrived at Rawhide; I and another guy named Jessie (who also was accepted into the About Face Program) entered through the visitation area. Upon our arrival, we greeted a few staff members, walked up some stairs, and then entered through another door; and once we were on the other side of that door, all I remember saying to myself was "wow"—and then it was confirmed that where I was standing would be my living quarters for the next 120 days.

Jessie and I arrived during suppertime, when all the guys and staff were gathered at the table, surrounded by delicious-looking food. At that moment, I was still in awe. We were both greeted and introduced to the rest of the cadets and staff; then, after supper, Jessie and I received our uniforms and other items and were escorted to our rooms. When it was time for curfew and almost lights out, I greeted my other roommates nervously, as this was all new to me. There I was in a beautiful home which I thought was the abode of the staff, but it was where *everyone* stayed. What a transition—from being locked in a 9'x10' room to having a room with a lot of space (which seemed like freedom). I can recall my new roommates telling me what to expect in the morning during roll call, and what to say. I can remember practicing all night, but when morning came and it was time to report, I still messed up. When it was my turn, I was nervous, yet had just enough guts to say (as my voice trembled), "Recruit reporting for duty"—though I was supposed to say, "Recruit Martin reporting for duty as ordered, Sir."

Man, do I remember my first day of PT (physical training)! We had to take a physical fitness test; I thought my heart was going to burst out of my chest, because it was beating so fast after the test. That night, while lying in my bunk in pain, I prayed to God, telling Him that I needed Him and thinking, *There is no way that I am going to be able to make it through this demanding program without Him.* I was out of shape physically, emotionally, and spiritually. I was going to need someone who was bigger and stronger than myself to help me through this trying time—so I surrendered myself to Him, saying, *Here I am; take me and use me.*

This is a practice that must be put to use first. We have to hand it all over to God by relinquishing ourselves to Him, and not just partially; we need to give of our whole beings (mind, body, and soul) in order for God to effectively work, do His part, and use us, shaping us into what He wants us to be. We have to be sold out for the Lord and no one else. We need to have appetites to give ourselves away and let the Lord know that we are giving ourselves to Him. Besides, our lives belong to Him anyway; His giving us free will just gives us the opportunity and choice to see whom we are going to serve in our lives. This must be done voluntarily. There is nothing worse than having someone give up something unwillingly.

> I was out of shape physically, emotionally, and spiritually. I was going to need someone who was bigger and stronger than myself to help me through this trying time—so I surrendered myself to Him, saying, Here I am; take me and use me.

For God to work His magic in us, we must also understand the enemy—Satan. He will try to throw obstacles in our way to distract us. But the truth of the matter is that he will only succeed if God is not in control of our lives. I can only speak for myself, but I cannot even imagine living without God in my life again; I have been there and done that (allowing Satan free reign of my actions), only to fall flat on my face! I cannot stress this enough that when we give ourselves to God, we must do so wholeheartedly. When this is the case, He will be able to use us in the way that He knows how, working in our best interests. Speaking from experience, I can guarantee that He will have our backs, if we allow Him to do so. I know what it feels like to be abandoned and left all alone, having had to fend for myself many times; it is no fun at all—as a matter of fact, it is a lonely and depressing road to travel. But God promises never to leave us or forsake us (see Hebrews 13:5-6).

So what does God mean by that? What He means is that we do not need to depend on these earthly, materialistic, and tangible things or humankind in times of need, because those things and people will let us down and disappoint us. We must just lean and depend on Him, because He will not leave us hangin'. Basically what God is saying is that when we allow Him entry into our lives and hearts, we never have to journey alone. All He requires is that we give ourselves away to Him; then He will take it from there! We must not dare think for a second of what others are going to say or think about us, because that is where we fail as well; we each need to live life to please the almighty God—because no one has a heaven or hell to put us in but ourselves and God.

KEY QUOTE

"Though my natural instinct is to wish for a life free from pain, trouble, and adversity, I am learning to welcome anything that makes me conscious of my need for Him. If prayer is birthed out of desperation, then anything that makes me desperate for God is a blessing"

~Nancy Leigh DeMoss

KEY VERSE

"For I know the plans that I have for you," declares the Lord, "Plans to prosper you and not to harm you, plans to give you hope and a future. Then you will call upon me and come and pray to me, and I will listen to you. You will seek me and find me when you seek me with all your heart. I will be found by you," declares the Lord, "and will bring you back from captivity. I will gather you from all the nations and places where I have banished you," declares the Lord, "and will bring you back to the place from which I carried you into exile."

—Jeremiah 29:11-14 (NIV)

Notes

Notes

Notes

Chapter 3

We Fall Down: Reaching to God for Forgiveness

Another way that the enemy will distract us from God is to use his advocates as obstacles on our paths—and it is their job to entertain us in many ways. I have witnessed the enemy's attacks on many occasions, from his regurgitating my past failures to his relishing in my present actions. The advocate will attempt to judge us as Christians and give us a definition of what a Christian ought to be, according to "society." What society has done is construct a "Christians" job description, and if an individual does not follow this particular job description, then he or she is not a "Christian" but a hypocrite: he or she is a faking "Christian," a "wannabe Christian." Trust me, I have heard it all before, but what members of society do not realize is that they are on the outside looking in, lacking the insight to even grasp what we have going on with God. Society says that we (Christians) are not in the position to fall down or sin, because we are Christians. However, we will have a hard time accomplishing such a task as living up to this bogus definition and profile of what a Christian ought to be.

As Christians, we will fall down (sin), but the good news is that we can reach out to God for forgiveness. In Him, we have redemption (deliverance and salvation) through His blood and the remission (forgiveness) of our offenses (shortcomings and trespasses)—in accordance with the riches and the generosity of His gracious favor (see Ephesians 1:17). When and if we fall down, the only possible mistakes that we could make are for us not to reach out to God, ask for His forgiveness, and repent. Oftentimes when we do fall down, instead of reaching to God we tend to reach out to the wrong "fixes," such as drugs, alcohol, sexual relationships, family, friends, and—for some—death (suicide). Those resources are only temporary "fixes." When it is all said and done, our "fix" should be Jesus; He is the only cure to heal our broken hearts and the only solution to our problems and/or dilemmas.

Many times, we have a propensity to use Jesus as our last resort, for whatever the reason. But when it comes to *my* situations, I now put Jesus toward the front, especially when I am facing trials and tribulations and my back is against the wall. I look to Jesus for advice, clarity, and understanding—and I can assure others that He has an active and open ear. However, I refuse to assert that everything is going to go right and smoothly when individuals give themselves to God; the truth is that this is precisely the time when the enemy begins to get frustrated and busy, and tries to come against believers with every scheme, attack, lie, and trickery he has up his sleeve. He will do any- and everything in his power to win over believers and persuade us not to obey the will of God. So on the occasions when we happen to trip up and fall into the trap, we need only ask for forgiveness and turn from that sin; it is just that simple—because we serve a forgiving God.

> When and if we fall down, the only possible mistakes that we could make are for us not to reach out to God, ask for His forgiveness, and repent.

While I was in the About Face Program at Rawhide, I learned the true purpose of the program. In the military, when you are told to do an about-face, you are supposed to make a 180-degree turn. The program was geared toward helping young men to accomplish and successfully do an "about-face" in life; whether it was the spiritual, emotional, or physical aspect of his journey in which an about-face was needed, the program was designed to assist him.

I remember an incident that occurred one time after I went back to my hometown while still enrolled in college. After I got home, I started a journey to Milwaukee and while en route, I ended up in a traffic jam on the interstate. I could not understand why this was so—having forgotten that there was construction work under way on that particular stretch of road. I remember asking myself, *Dang, they still working on this interstate?* The thing that I must remember was that in order for the interstate to be constructed correctly, it took time and patience. Plus, it was a major project for that interstate, due to all the work that was being put into it and what would be the finished product, in comparison to what it was like prior to the construction. To be honest, there will always be some type of construction being done on that interstate, considering the maintenance for normal wear and tear. This story serves as a parallel to how I look at our lives. We are projects which are under construction, and there are going to be some areas in our lives that are rough and some that are smooth; we just have to realize that as works continually in progress, even when we think that certain facets of our beings are completed, God may come in and begin other projects in our lives that need our attention—according to His plans for our lives.

> I refuse to assert that everything is going to go right and smoothly when individuals give themselves to God; the truth is that this is precisely the time when the enemy begins to get frustrated and busy, and tries to come against believers with every scheme, attack, lie, and trickery he has up his sleeve.

Every day when I pray, I ask the Lord to forgive me for any sins that I may have committed against Him; no matter if I was aware of them or not, I still ask for His forgiveness. As Christians, we have to build our relationship with God. We can do so just by taking time and spending it with Him—just us and Him. And we must not be ashamed of having a relationship with Him. The Bible teaches us that whosoever is ashamed of Jesus is ashamed of the Father and shall not get into the kingdom.

I remember that while watching an episode of *Law and Order: SVU* on television, a particular scene grabbed my attention (as usual): A little boy was riding his bicycle in front of his house. His father came to check on him and told him to make sure that he rode his bicycle in front of the house and nowhere else. Well, after a few minutes had elapsed, the little boy decided to ride to the street corner and back; but upon riding back, he ended up falling off his bike after hitting a crack in the sidewalk. He cried aloud; his father heard his cry: "Daddy, help!" The father rushed outside to see what was wrong, only to find his son lying on the ground, gripping his arm. The boy's father came to his aid and saw that the boy was going to be all right, that he only had a scrape on his arm. The little boy reached out for his daddy to pick him up and daddy did; then the little boy said to his daddy, "Daddy, I'm sorry"—to which the father looked at his son and responded, "Son, just don't do it again."

I relay that story because it reminds me of our relationship with Jesus: even when we are in the wrong, the good news is that we can go to Him and say, "Father, forgive me," and He will—without passing judgment on us. One of my favorite stories in the Bible comes from John 8:1-11, concerning the woman who was caught in adultery and brought before Jesus. My favorite verse of this particular passage is verse 7 (NIV), when Jesus told her accusers, "If any one of you is without sin, let him be the first to throw a stone at her." If you heard or read the story before, then you know that those accusers began to slowly walk away, one at a time. Then the story goes on to read that Jesus asked the woman if anyone had condemned her and that she replied no, so Jesus told her that He also would not condemn her, and to go and leave her life of sin. This is the type of God we serve—a forgiving and loving God.

The Bible teaches us that "all have sinned and fall short of the glory of God" (Romans 3:23, NIV). Christians are sinners saved by grace, and as such, if we do happen to fumble or get caught up in the midst of wrongdoing, we must remember that we serve a God who is a merciful God, willing and ready to forgive us. Many of us may remember when we first began to ride a bicycle; well, in my opinion, living life is somewhat similar to learning how to ride a bike. Some children had their first bike ride with training wheels attached to their mode of transportation, but I learned how to ride a bike (without training wheels) by way of one of my cousins holding on to the back of the seat and then pushing me and letting go. What I also remember about those moments is that when I was riding the bike without any assistance, I would keep my balance only for a moment and then I would fall; and when I would fall, I would scramble to get up, trying to save myself from the embarrassment of having another human being witness my fall. Thus, I would get back up and try it again, only to fall again. I was persistent in learning how to ride a bike—spills and all—until I learned what I needed to do to have a steady and smooth biking experience.

Some of us may consider this to be an accurate depiction of how life is lived: held only for so long in order to gain balance, and then released into the wind of life. If I can just keep it real, life seems to follow the same pattern, because once you turn eighteen (and for some it may be either earlier or later), you are getting prepared for life and that is when learning to ride with the training wheels or by being pushed and then released come into play. Some learners are given training wheels, meaning that they are being prepped for life by mother and/or father, or whomever, in order to ensure that correct decisions are being made and to protect them from falling; nevertheless, they, too, will experience life without the training wheels when the time is right—because no one wants to depend on training wheels for the remainder of his or her life. But the ones who were just pushed and then let go to brave life (because they did not have the luxury of having training wheels) had to just endure the falling and embarrassment; however, surprisingly, the falling and embarrassment are what shaped and molded them into who they are.

> Then the story goes on to read that Jesus asked the woman if anyone had condemned her and that she replied no, so Jesus told her that He also would not condemn her,

Even when we fall, we must get up and continue to ride, keeping in mind that "practice makes perfect." When we do fall down in life (i.e., make a mistake or misstep), we must acknowledge the mistake, ask God for forgiveness, and keep it moving. I discovered that we can keep ourselves down by caring about what others are going to think of us because we have fallen down. I can admit that I used to care about what others thought of me because of my past mistakes in life, but I had to realize that humankind has no heaven or hell in which to place me and that, due to Jesus' presence in my life, I was beginning a new journey.

Thanks go to God for being a forgiving God, who shows us grace and compassion as His children. And one way that He exhibits these qualities is by enabling us to surround ourselves with people who will assist us in picking ourselves up and dusting ourselves off when we fall. I remember times when I surrounded myself with individuals who would try to kick me when I was down; it soon became obvious that these are not the type of people that we should include in our support systems. And having a crowd of folks make up our support systems is not necessarily a must; a few strong, rooted, and anchored peers would do the job just fine. This is not to say that we should frown upon having a large support system; it has its benefits. But the more people we allow to get close to us, the better chance we have of someone eventually dropping us or leaving us hanging when we need him or her most.

That is why it is important to have that "faithful few"—those whom we know would not and will not leave us hanging. But no one can replace the security of God, so we must always put our trust in God, who will never leave us or forsake us. If and when we do fall down, we are to reach up to God so that He can pick us up…it will never be too late.

KEY QUOTE

"God invented forgiving as a remedy for a past that not even He could change and not even He could forget. His way of forgiving is the model for our forgiving."

~Lewis B. Smedes

KEY VERSE

I acknowledged my sin to You, and my iniquity I did not hide; I said, "I will confess my transgressions to the Lord"; And You forgave the guilt of my sin.

—Psalm 32:5 (NASB)

Notes

Notes

Notes

Chapter 4

He Saw the Best in Me: Realizing God's Favor upon Your Life

If a person is in the position to read this book, then the truth of the matter is that he or she is favored. How? Well, this person need only think back to where God has brought him or her from and trace the events up to where he or she currently is in his or her life. Truth be told, if there are some of us who cannot see the difference between life with God and life without God, then perhaps those people are not being honest with themselves.

I know that when it comes to *my* life and my being a child of God, I am *highly* favored by God. Even though I do not deserve to be a recipient of His favor, He still showers it upon me. I am so glad that I did not take to heart what others said about me—even though *some* of it may have been true. Just knowing who I was in the sight of God (not considering what humankind thought of me) prompted me to realize God's favor upon my life. I really felt hopeless upon discovering that the ones whom I surrounded myself with, thinking they were there to help me, really did not have my best interests at heart, especially since they only focused on the bad in me instead of the good. To be fair, not even *I* had my own well-being in mind. In all honesty, it was not that I wanted to continue to do the things that I was doing—it was just that my living that lifestyle was really all I knew how to do in order to survive in life. There were times when I even felt about myself the way others felt about me; I allowed what others were saying to me and about me to invade my thoughts as truth. Thus, I truly started to believe that I was not going to achieve anything in life.

When I was at Ethan Allen, I really thought that my life was over and that it was not going to be worth anything after my stint there. While there, I had, once again, given up on my faith in God, because reality had set in that I was *really* there. I did not know what God was working out on my behalf—all I knew was that I was locked up and did not know where my life was headed from that moment.

> I am so glad that I did not take to heart what others said about me—even though some of it may have been true. Just knowing who I was in the sight of God (not considering what humankind thought of me) prompted me to realize God's favor upon my life.

What I was experiencing in my life then was true favor (I just did not know it). For example, how is it that I got waived into adult court, then (and this part remains a mystery to me) the decision was reversed and I got waived back into the juvenile courts and ended up in Ethan Allen Juvenile Correctional Facility? I could have wound up in an adult facility, but the favor of God was upon me, allowing me the luxury of not even having to catch a glimpse inside of an adult facility.

But, wait, that was not all: God allowed for me to go to Rawhide—a Christian-based organization; out of all the programs of which I could have been a part, God had seen fit for me to be at Rawhide. It was at Rawhide where I received discipline and the rest of the independent living skills needed for my going out on my own. After all the favor He had shown me, God was still in the giving mood, because after leaving Rawhide's Independent Living Program, I was able to get into another independent-living program that assisted me in paying my rent, my utilities, and other such things—even when I was not in the county where it was set up. The program was in Kenosha and I was in Racine; and the program was actually geared toward teens and young adults who lived in that county, but somehow (favor), it worked out for me to get accepted into the program.

So after a couple of years, God was at it again, blessing me by allowing me to go to college; and, to add the icing on the cake, I was able to attend debt-free, without having to take out a loan or anything. These circumstances were made possible by churches, professors, and other donors whom God used to help me be successful in my schooling. These persons and institutions saw beyond my past transgressions and into the future of what God had planned for me, as one of His children.

I am one of God's children (as are all believers)—and it does not matter what neighborhoods we are from or where we were raised, what our names are, who our parents or families are, what our sexuality or sexual orientation is, where we work (because at least we have jobs), what schools we attend(ed), what brand of clothing we wear, what we have done, what is on our criminal records, and so forth. What society has done is use those details as name tags through which to identify who we are and where we are supposed to end up in life; but, that is a lie from the pits of hell—for what God has for us, is for us. We, the people, have bought into this notion and entertained it for such a long period of time that we have adopted and adapted to this social stigma, thus misidentifying ourselves and who we really are. Some of us have been brainwashed straight into our graves (suicide), or to the point where we have given up on life and are content with our current statuses in life.

But instead of being complacent in the world, we must stand up and be proud of who we really are as children of God, realizing that we are favored. It feels so good to confirm that I am one (of many thousands of young African-American males) who is being productive with his life instead of being incarcerated and/or in somebody's cemetery, as statistics predicted.

Statistics state that African Americans like me should be dead or incarcerated for life because of where we live and our pasts, ages, and ethnicities. Join me and other young men and women in proving society and our so-called department of justice wrong—from the White House to the very courtrooms which convict our fellow young men and women every day. As I look back over my life and see who I was then and to whom I have been transformed, I cannot help but to give God some praise. I could have or should have been dead or locked up under somebody's jail cell a long time ago, but it is because of God's recipe for my life (a little bit of grace, mercy, favor, and love) that I was able to escape those circumstances.

So, how do we realize God's favor upon our lives? Well, I would have to call Sister Sarah to the witness stand to testify of God's favor upon her life and what she had to do in order to realize it. Sarah was well past childbearing age, so she started to run her mouth, which caused her not to be in agreement with God. One might ask Sarah, "Sarah, isn't it true that you had a little talk with Jesus and believed on Him in your heart, and that's when God's favor began to manifest itself by allowing you to get pregnant? So you're saying that all you had to do was conceive in your heart of who you are—a child of God—and that God is capable and able to do the possible as well as the impossible?"

> It feels so good to confirm that I am one (of many thousands of young African-American males) who is being productive with his life instead of being incarcerated and/or in somebody's cemetery, as statistics predicted.

Just as we may question the faith of people like Sarah, who are in the position to doubt things that God says because they seem far-fetched or outlandish, we have the tendency to question God's favor upon our lives; just because He is not moving or responding in the way we would like for Him to do does not necessarily mean that He is not working on our behalf. Often, we are the root causes of some of the situations and messes we tend to face, simply because we interrupted or interfered in God's plan for our lives. We must attempt to at least try to understand God, who has a way of setting up our lives according to His will and not ours; He has a way of strategically placing people, places, and things, and/or taking away the very same from our lives—so that we may discover His favor upon our lives.Or He may just be trying to get our attention and give us a reality check.

I remember my freshman year at American Baptist College (Holy Hill). I will never forget this particular incident, which, until it actually happened, was a scenario that I had never contemplated.

My professor had asked us to give the meanings of a skill and a talent, in our own words. I had always assumed they meant the same thing, so I attempted to look in the dictionary to see what both words meant, which did not lead to more insight. Thus, when it was time for me to give my response, I gave as simple and shallow a response as my fellow classmates.

That experience prompted the beginning of my having to think critically and outside the box. The professor broke down to us what each word meant and how easy it was for each to get confused with the other. He taught us that a skill is something to be learned, something that can be taught—whereas a talent is a gift, something that already exists inside of us. For some, it may take a while for them to even notice their gift, but it is there. We must be encouraged that God has given all of His children a talent; and He wants us to use our talents for His sake so that in the end, He will get all the glory.

> Often, we are the root causes of some of the situations and messes we tend to face, simply because we interrupted or interfered in God's plan for our lives.

Each of us may wonder, "What is my purpose in life?" We must be able to realize our life's purpose and where we want to go in life. We must not make our decisions based on what others want us to do; we must decide based on where we want to go in life and determine what we truly feel to be our purposes on planet earth. Yes, it is a daunting task for one to realize his or her life's purpose, just as it took me a while to realize what my purpose was. When we figure out our purposes, we have to do what we need to do in order to bring them to fruition. We must not worry about our past failures—only press on toward the future.

Another one of our biggest mistakes is to get in our own way of success and our life's purpose. We just have to tell ourselves, "Get out of the way, I'm coming through!" I reminisce all the time about where I could have been and should have been. I know that while I did not understand my getting waived into the adult court, only to have that decision reversed and get to be restored to juvenile status, I can now recognize how that circumstance was favor. God will show up and show out on our behalves by supplying what our hearts desire. With that being said, if we do our part, then God will do His.

Remember, it is the enemy's job to deter us and get our minds off of Jesus; folks are going to lie on us, call us ungodly names, rebel against us, and attempt to steal our joy, happiness, and hope—but we must stay strong in the Lord and call on Him during those hard and difficult times (for He will answer us). The Bible teaches us that all things work out for the good of those who love God and are called according to His purpose (see Romans 8:28).

> He taught us that a skill is something to be learned, something that can be taught—whereas a talent is a gift, something that already exists inside of us. For some, it may take a while for them to even notice their gift, but it is there.

KEY QUOTE

"I have no regrets in my life. I think that everything happens to you for a reason. The hard times that you go through build character, making you a stronger person."

~Rita Moreno

KEY VERSE

In him we were also chosen, having been predestined according to the plan of him who works out everything in conformity with the purpose of his will.

—Ephesians 1:11 (NIV)

Notes

Notes

Notes

Chapter 5

Never Would Have Made It: Recognizing the Source of Our Strength

I was in first or second grade when I learned about the source of energy and how it was involved in the growth of the trees, plants, and grass. I would imagine that most of us learned this information sometime during the elementary school years or some other relevant point in life. I remember the lesson in science class (or the science portion of the day) about energy and the things involved in helping the grass, flowers, trees, fruits, vegetables, and other things to grow.

Many elements play a role in the growth of each creation, but there is one particular thing needed in order for the product to actually begin to live and have strength—the sun. My science teacher assigned my class a project to do in order to show and prove to us that this was true. We had to plant a small tree inside of a six-ounce Styrofoam cup. The teacher showed us her completed project and what our trees should look like after completion. I was in awe and had to see it for myself, being of the age when that type of stuff amazed me. So, we got our materials ready so we could get our project on and "crackin'": the dirt, water, the cup, and the seed to plant.

After we planted the seed inside the dirt contained in the Styrofoam cups, the teacher told us to write our names on our cups and set our cups on the window sill. A few days later (and daily watering), I went to check on mine—but nothing was there; I was beginning to get discouraged and thought that my plant was not going to grow. I thought I had done something wrong, but the teacher ensured the class that some take longer than others to sprout, and that it would take a while for us to begin to see the plants grow. So, after a few *more* days of sunshine and watering, I noticed a stem sprouting with a tiny leaf on it. I still felt as though my plant was developmentally challenged or something, because it was taking so long to grow. I started to look around at others' projects, observing that they were growing faster than mine; so, I moved mine to a different area on the window sill—but still nothing. Then one day, after I had given up hope that my plant would bloom, my pitiful little seedling grew into a plant.

I did not understand the process then, but I do now. If it had not been for the sun, shining down on that plant, the plant would have never grown. If I could project the picture through my spiritual lenses, the characters would be as follows: Christians would be the seed; the world would be the cup; our heartaches, pain, tears, and sleepless nights would be the dirt; and hope (faith) would be the water and Jesus, the sun. We are a part of this world—and as sure as we are alive, at some point we will experience or have already experienced some type of heartache, pain, tears, and sleepless nights.

So, here we are in this world full of pain and heartache; even in the midst of troubles, we are able to grow. Our faith helps to ease our pain, by reminding us that it is not over yet—because the sun (Jesus) still needs to shine and put His final touches on the situation. After many days of storms, finally the Son arrives to shine upon us. I guess He did keep His promise: He said that He will never leave us or forsake us. My life serves as a testament to this fact. In reminiscing about the place where I was reared to all the mess I had gotten myself into, I know that I could not have made it without

Jesus, who was my strength when I felt like giving up and throwing in the towel (because my life seemed purposeless and hopeless). But it is during those times of despair and doubt that God works best. He wants us to build our faith and hope in Him—and that is precisely how I made it: I had put my hope in Him and He turned my situation around thusly, providing hope in a hopeless situation.

When I drive up and down the streets of Nashville, I witness the individuals (panhandlers) on the side of the road asking for money or food via signs that basically read, "Hopeless, can you help?" As I look at those signs, I just start to ponder how many men and women are holding up those signs around the country. Then I ask myself if they have to be holding up those signs in order to indicate that they are hopeless and need help. The answer is that there are thousands of people who are holding those signs yet do not realize they are doing so. I am talking about that teen mother and father who decided to have a few minutes of pleasure which resulted in a child, and now they both consider life to be hopeless. Or how about the young man or woman who was raised around nothing but partying, drugs, and alcohol—hence, that is all he or she knows; as a result, all he or she does is club, drink, and "420" (marijuana) all day, after deciding to drop out of school because he or she felt as though there was no hope—that he or she is too far in to get out.

I can witness to putting my hope and faith into different things just so that I may experience a quick turnaround in my situation; but instead, the situation just got worse or I ended up failing, because it was only a temporary fix—a treatment instead of a cure. Some of us may be putting our faith and hope in the wrong thing, leaving us feeling desperate, lonely, helpless, and abandoned, which leads to the ultimate feeling of hopelessness. When we recognize that Jesus is the source of our strength, we can overcome any obstacle that is put in our way and have victory over our lives. Something that is very important to remember is that there is nobody greater than Jesus; just ask those who have searched for other answers rather than going to the only source who can actually solve their problems (they will tell us the same).

I remember how one time, back in seventh grade, my math teacher gave us a pop quiz which I had not studied for, though she had given the class fair warning about it the previous week. Being unprepared, I decided to look onto the paper of a classmate who happened to have studied for the quiz. Well, to make a long story short, the teacher had given everyone the same questions—just not in the same numerical order. So, yeah, of course I failed the test and had to retake it; plus, I received a sixty-minute detention because she wrote me up. The moral of that story was that I was going about succeeding in the wrong way, instead of studying for myself and learning the correct answers.

> When we recognize that Jesus is the source of our strength, we can overcome any obstacle that is put in our way and have victory over our lives.

In other words, when we take shortcuts, those paths only lead to temporary success—that is it. I was always told to do something right the first time in order to avoid having to do it a second time. I sure wish I would have heeded those wise words at different junctures in my life; I could have saved myself from a great deal of heartache and disappointment. Well, what is done is done, but what I have come to realize is that if it had not been for the Son, Jesus, I would not have grown to be the man I am today.

KEY QUOTE
"The more we depend on God the more dependable we find He is."
~Cliff Richard

KEY VERSE
I can do all things through him who strengthens me.
—Philippians 4:13 (NRSV)

Notes

Notes

Notes

Chapter 6

Prayed Up: Regular Rapport with God

As a youngster, it was difficult for me to pray because I did not know how to do so; I was embarrassed to pray in public, in front of others. Do not get me wrong, I was not shy or anything, but I was afraid that I would be judged and laughed at because I did not know the "lingo" of the church. To this day, I cannot believe how ignorant I was about prayer; prayer is just a form of communication between us and God—that is all. But back then, I did not know whether He would hear my prayer or not—until I got caught up in some mess and I could not call on anyone else. It was then that the words of my Sunday school teacher seemed to echo in my ears: "Just call His name, Jesus, and He will hear you." Well, I was left with no options but to call on the name which is above all names—Jesus.

Let me make it clear that that was probably the best decision I had/have ever made. I do not know how, but I seemed to walk away from the mess unscathed, having only been left with my thoughts and curiosity about how it was possible to do so. How did the problem go

> ...prayer is just a form of communication between us and God.

away? I found myself going crazy, trying to understand God and how He works. But really, all I needed to know was that I am His child, whom He loves, and that I am an unfinished product (still in the making).

When I was incarcerated at Ethan Allen, there was a chaplain there named Reverend Cole; I remember meeting with him, discussing my loneliness and my not being able to sleep. He ended up asking me one simple question which allowed me to establish a true and authentic relationship with Jesus; he asked, "Do you have a relationship with Jesus?" I sat there, pondering his question, after which I responded by saying, "I don't know." Chaplain Cole then explained to me what it meant to have a relationship with Jesus; after hearing his explanation, I accepted Jesus back into my life, and this time I connected with Him by talking to Him daily.

Pastor Cole asked whether I had a best friend and I told him that I did. Then he asked if we had a good, healthy friendship; I said yes. Next, he asked if my best friend could tell me and ask me for anything and vice versa; I again said yes. Finally, he asked if my best friend was here with me at that moment; I thought he was trying to be funny—but all he was doing was trying to make a point that Jesus is with us at all times and that I could go to Him morning, noon, and, night. He enlightened me to build that type of relationship with Jesus: talk to Him, ask Him questions. Chaplain Cole reminded me that I was a child of God—that old things are passed away and all things become new.

It was at that point that I could finally have peace of mind, even though I was where I was in the physical realm. But now I am who I am: a new creature. In this new relationship with Jesus, I found myself feeling better and having a sense of freedom—even though I was locked up physically (though not spiritually and emotionally). During those times when I would get lonely and stare at the pictures of my family, suddenly I would feel God's company. He would tell me that I would see them soon and that I just needed to hold on. Now I know why my grandmother (Dorothy Rae Martin) would say that He is a company keeper in the midnight hour, because in my darkest moments He would/will be there, when everyone else had/has disappeared and abandoned me.

During times when I am feeling weak and hopeless, He is right there beside me. I am sure many (if not all) of us have succumbed to peer pressure before. Peer pressure occurs when one has a so-called friend who is trying to persuade him or her to do something that is against his or her better judgment, or that the individual knows is not in his or her best interest. There is always one person in the clique who eventually walks away from the situation and decides not to be part of the plan—yet some way, somehow, ends up getting him- or herself involved. Inevitably, the idea that originally seemed to be a good one in the minds of the group members ended up being a bad decision made by all persons involved—leaving regret in its wake. That is why it is so important for us as children of God to consistently talk with Jesus; otherwise, the enemy will sneak in and say what he has to say in our ears and hearts.

Needless to say, there will always be consequences for our actions. Yes, God will punish us for making the wrong decision, but His disciplining us is for our good in the long run. We have to understand that there is spiritual warfare going on, and that at no time can we depend on our fleshly and human abilities to win this battle; we are just not strong enough to do so. That is why we need to be strong enough spiritually to go to Jesus, who will give us the power that we need.

Besides, who do we think we are that we decide we donot need to pray? Any time we harbor that type of attitude or cockiness, we will fall straight into the enemy's hands—because that is how he wants us to think and feel. Even Jesus, when He stepped into humanness, constantly went to the Mount of Olives to pray, not only for Himself, but also for His disciples and the people of God. Jesus always kept an active communication between Himself and God, because He knew that He needed somebody stronger than He to intercede on His behalf.

> That is why it is so important for us as children of God to consistently talk with Jesus; otherwise, the enemy will sneak in and say what he has to say in our ears and hearts.

In Luke 22, Jesus was preparing to face the hour of His crucifixion; but even while He was readying Himself, still He was trying to teach His disciples another thing or two. The first thing that He was trying to teach them was how to overcome temptation;

and the second was to obey the will of God. These two things were to be done through prayer. In Luke 22:40 (NIV), this is what Jesus told His disciples: "Pray that you will not fall into temptation." Jesus knew that the enemy was prowling and trying to devour His disciples, so He encouraged them to pray so that they may not fall into the enemy's snare of temptation.

Only through prayer can we remain faithful to our purpose and mission in life. Upon further reading of Luke 22 (verse 41), we learn that Jesus went by Himself to pray: "Father, if you are willing, take this cup from me" (verse 42, NIV). In these verses, Jesus shows us how to pray and come to the holy Father in reverence—when faced with distress, depression, pain, suffering, haters, and everything else that would bring us to the point of feeling hopeless (ready to throw in the towel). See, when Jesus was praying to God to take away the cup (pain, agony, burdens, and so forth), He was praying for God's plan to change.

That may sound familiar to us: going to God in prayer, actually trying to change the plan—which in essence means trying to change the will of God. But God leaves us in these situations for a reason. He does not just do things just for the sake of doing them; He has the plan put together for us *and* Him. Even though Jesus requested for God to take the cup from Him, God responded to His request by sending an angel to give Jesus the strength that He needed in order to endure what He was about to face.

When we are running low on strength, we need only go to Jesus so that He can give us strength to keep on keeping on—because we are going to be faced with more haters, pain, sleepless nights, liars, and more. But all we need to keep in mind is that we have the strength from Almighty God to overcome anything in life. I know that there probably will be times when it seems as though God is not listening; but the truth of the matter is that He is listening, just waiting to see if we are going to keep Him informed of that which He already knows.

Now I know why the mothers in the church would always say that God may not come when we want Him to, but He is always on time. We have to stop thinking that Jesus is on our time and must answer when we say answer, because it does not even work like that. I do apologize if I have offended anyone in any way, fashion, or form with my words, but we have been misinformed way too long now and somebody must stand up and say that enough is enough. We (as a new and evolving generation of believers) must be able to keep each other informed and educated on the topic of Christianity. I will tell you this: Christianity is not just something that we can put on and then take off whenever we want to do so; being a Christian really is a full-time job—plus overtime. But God equips His children with the necessary tools to complete any task that we are given.

KEY QUOTE

"There is not in the world a kind of life more sweet and delightful than that of a continual conversation with God."

~Brother Lawrence Bell

KEY VERSE

Evening, and morning, and at noon, will I pray, and cry aloud: and he shall hear my voice.

—Psalm 55:17 (KJV)

Notes

Notes

Notes

Chapter 7

Smile: Retain Your Faith

When people come into contact with someone who seems unhappy or troubled, they may feel obliged to say, "Smile, it will get better." Or perhaps they provide the person with this tidbit of information: "It takes a greater number of facial muscles to frown than it does to smile." Many of us may have been in a situation where we were upset and angry at someone, and either that individual or someone around would say or do something that was funny, causing us to laugh and smile—thus forgetting why we were even upset in the first place.

Is it possible for a person to be in a situation or dilemma that causes him or her to be upset, angry, mad and so forth, yet happy, silly, and excited at the same time? Well, maybe we have never lived this circumstance, but I have found myself at times asking how I can have a smile in times such as these; how I can smile when I feel as though my world is coming to an end; how I can smile when I am facing persecution; how I can smile when my world is dark; how I can smile when I am hurting on the inside and feeling helpless and hopeless; how I can smile while I am experiencing this spirit of loneliness.

I have asked myself these questions many times when I thought I was experiencing seeming oxymoron circumstances, but really I was not. The Bible teaches us that we wrestle not against flesh and blood, but against spiritual principalities. The enemy wants us to react to dilemmas and difficult situations with our human nature, but as believers we have to remember the teachings of Jesus. He teaches us that in this world we have trouble, but we are to take heart and be of good cheer (smile)—for He has overcome the world (see John 16:33).

Jesus assured us that we would have some rough and tough times, but that we must keep the faith in Him, realizing that those rough and tough times are only temporary situations—because He has overcome every obstacle, trial, and tribulation that He comes across. The way we go about retaining our faith is by being obedient to God, loving our enemies, and praying for those who persecute us (see Romans 12:14). We can also bless those who are against us by praying for them (with a smile), and—as I remember hearing during childhood—by "killing them with kindness" (smile).

One incentive to smile is that we look better with smiles on our faces, despite the situations in which we find ourselves. We have no choice but to smile when we know that God is definitely in the midst of everything, ensuring that in the end we are going to be on top. We must remember that God is always working on our behalf, because we are His (God's) property and He will not allow bad things to happen to us. Some of us probably ask ourselves, "If God really loves me, then why is He allowing these types of things to happen to me? He is supposed to be keeping me safe, but it seems as though the enemy is attacking me from every way and direction."

This is the type of God we serve, though. He is a selfish God; He will place us in certain situations (when it seems as though all of our resources have been drained) just to see whether or not we will call on and have faith in Him when we get into these helpless

"Kill them with kindness" (smile).

and hopeless situations. If and when we do call on His name, we must not do so as a last resort; we will save ourselves from a lot of headaches and troubles when we just have faith and know that God always has our backs, even when we are the cause our own messes.

At different times in our lives, we tend to have the "Peter" type of faith: we are trying to stretch out our hands to God but lack the total faith which is due Him—taking our eyes off of Him and instead focusing our attention on our problems. Someone once told me that instead of telling God how BIG our mountains are, we need to tell our mountains how BIG our GOD is. We need to have faith like the woman whose daughter was demon-possessed. She was persistent in asking Jesus to have mercy, and for Him to heal her daughter; even when it seemed as though Jesus was ignoring her, she still was diligent in asking for His assistance. And when Jesus saw that the woman's faith was genuine, He said to her, "'Woman, you have great faith! Your request is granted.' And her daughter was healed from that very hour" (Matthew 15:28, NIV).

See, we really need to assess this woman's situation and the lengths to which she went in order to ensure that her daughter was healed. It is easy for me to tell others to have faith as this woman had, but we all must realize it for ourselves. This woman was a Gentile and Canaanite, and was not even supposed to be talking to Jesus, because there was a rivalry between the Jews and Canaanites. This is important to note, because it serves as proof that she was willing to be deemed an outcast because of her going to this Jew and asking for His help. Wow, that is faith!

She then took it a step further to show how serious she was: she knelt down in front of Jesus, begging Him to heal her daughter. Even after this act, though it seemed like an even more hopeless situation—it appeared as though Jesus was ignoring her—the woman kept her faith and did not give up until she got what she had asked for. That is all Jesus wants from us: for us to have genuine faith and be persistent in trusting in Him, even when it seems as though Jesus is ignoring us. We must trust that He will come in and turn our situations around. Plus, while it may seem that some of our situations are hurting us, God is working everything out for our good. I think that is why God leaves us in certain predicaments for undisclosed periods of time: He does this just so we can have these experiences.

To me, life is all about experiences and how we make the best of them. I remember when I was attending American Baptist College and collaborated with several other college students on a project that took place on the campus of Fisk University in Nashville, Tennessee; there were about seven of us from different colleges. One day, when we were finishing our meeting, one student from a very prestigious school in Nashville asked where we were going to have lunch; some did not know—some did know. The ones who knew what they wanted recommended McDonald's, prompting one student to inquire, "Don't y'all get tired of going there?" Well, as I was part of the group that wanted McDonald's, I responded to his question with, "No, it's all we have enough [money] for." The student replied, "I don't see how y'all do it," and that he could not eat there as often as we did. He said that he was going to eat at Five Guys on West End Ave., and that we should join him; again, we told him that we did not have "Five Guys" money in our budget and that that was not the time to splurge.

In quite a serious manner, the guy replied that we have to be open to the opportunity to try quality food one day, that that very same day was our day to do so, and that he was going to treat everyone. Feeling ashamed, we declined the offer and went our separate ways. The group that wanted McDonald's went there and ate, and while we were eating we put our heads together to try to figure out what "Mr. Big Shot" was getting at: Was he really trying to treat us as though we were charity cases? Based on his testimonies of how he and his family had donated to many organizations and how he really had not struggled in life, this seemed like a no-brainer.

What Mr. Big Shot may not have realized is that I had been struggling all my life, so my not being able to splurge on a regular basis or live beyond my means did not faze me. Plus, having to dine at McDonald's and other like places was not anything new to me; I ate it when I was young and continue to eat it to this day. I feel as though I have a passion for struggle; I appreciate experiencing trying times, because then I know how to handle myself when faced with the same problems or dilemmas. I will not be trying to act "brand new" (like I don't know what's going on) in the situation—I can just keep on keeping on because I know how to overcome it.

Struggling has been a part of the black culture for ages; we (as a people) have always been struggling in life. Yet, after our overcoming a struggle, there always seems to be hope waiting for us with a smile. Those who have a banking or savings account in either a credit union or bank may ask themselves whether or not their money is really safe in these financial institutions, and whether they would have access to their funds if the financial institution were to meet its demise. I find it quite interesting to consider the fact that we deposit our money and assets into these institutions which are not guaranteed to give us a return on our investments—in the event they were to go bankrupt and/or out of business.

The only sure thing is that when we actually deposit our faith into God, He guarantees us that He will never leave us or forsake us. Faith means having confidence that God will keep His promises.

KEY QUOTE

"There is nothing that wastes the body like worry, and one who has any faith in God should be ashamed to worry about anything whatsoever."

~Mahatma Gandhi

KEY VERSE

Now faith is being sure of what we hope for and certain of what we do not see.

—Hebrews 11:1 (NIV)

Notes

Notes

Notes

Conclusion

My prayer is that this book has been and will be an inspiration to those who have read it or will read it. The overall purpose for this writing is to give others hope that no matter what happens in life, we can do all things through Christ Jesus, who gives us strength. Also, God knows how much we can take and He promises us that He will never put more on us than we can bear (see 1 Corinthians 10:13).

I will never forget my first sermon topic: "Hold On, You Can Overcome"; I used John 16:33 as a reference point—regarding when Jesus was telling His disciples that they were going to face some hard times but that they needed to hold on, take heart, and not worry (because He had overcome those obstacles which were before Him.

We must remember that we are children of God, who is the only one who can give us the power to navigate our destinies and futures. I guarantee that if we allow God to take control of our lives, then our hearts will surely be led in the right direction—because in Him, there is nothing but hope. No matter how low we sink in life (to where we believe there is no hope), the good news is that when we put our hands in God's hand and just hand our problems and worries over to Him, He handles the rest.

To those of us who have not given their lives to the Lord and who want Him to take control of their destinies and lives—who want Him to be their Lord and personal Savior—it is not too late to do so. They need only make a decision that they will never regret; I know that it is the best decision that I have ever made!

It is as simple as 1, 2, 3...just pray this simple prayer:

Dear Lord,

I am coming to you, admitting that I am a sinner. I have done things that I am sure that You did not care much for. I did me and now I want to live for You. I am sorry and I am asking for Your forgiveness. I believe that You died on the cross for me, to save me. You did something that was bold and real—and I appreciate it. I come to you to ask that You take control of my life; I give myself to You. Help me to live every day to please You, Lord. I love You and I thank You for allowing me to spend eternity with You. I am asking You into my life, to take control from this day forward—for only You can save me from my sins, because You are God. In Jesus' name I pray. Amen.

If you prayed that prayer of salvation, then you have been saved and born again; welcome my sister, welcome my brother—to a new life where there still is hope and a life full of promises. Romans 10:9 (NIV) reads, "If you confess with your mouth, 'Jesus is Lord,' and believe in your heart that God raised him from the dead, you will be saved."

I encourage every Christian (newly converted and otherwise) to find a God-centered, biblically based church that has sound preaching and teaching which will help him or her grow in his or her walk with Christ—a church to call home: one that accepts people for who they are and what they were.

~Smile, keep the faith, and do not give up…it is only a test!~

About the Author

Montreal Martin is a proud graduate of the American Baptist College in Nashville, Tennessee, having earned a Bachelor of Arts degree in Biblical Studies and Sociology. Martin is currently pursuing a Master of Divinity degree.

Martin has a passion for befriending, mentoring, and counseling today's youth and young adults. Many ask him why he would be involved in youth ministry, as these persons consider it to be a difficult ministry to endure. Martin believes that if God has called or ordained an individual to work in a certain area of ministry, then He equips him or her to endure anything! The challenges and hardships he faced as an adolescent compels him to currently reach out to at-risk young men and women today, letting them know that they are valuable in the eyes of God and that without Him, nothing is possible.

Additionally, since Martin is aware of the challenges and dilemmas that the youth are facing, he yearns to be a positive role model, mentor, and surrogate father in the lives of other young men and women. He is an advocate for bridging the intergenerational gap in the church and bringing the church back into the communities, which will ultimately bring the communities back into the church.

Despite the trials, troubles, and tests, Martin believes that there still is hope—when we have Jesus on our side.

Reverend Martin has been blessed to share his testimony by way of preaching and teaching in many diverse settings. Martin is a preacher, teacher, motivational speaker, active social justice advocate, and life mentor. He resides in Nashville, Tennessee.

www.ingramcontent.com/pod-product-compliance
Lightning Source LLC
Chambersburg PA
CBHW050605300426
44112CB00013B/2086